TO_____

FROM_____

ON_____

DATE_____

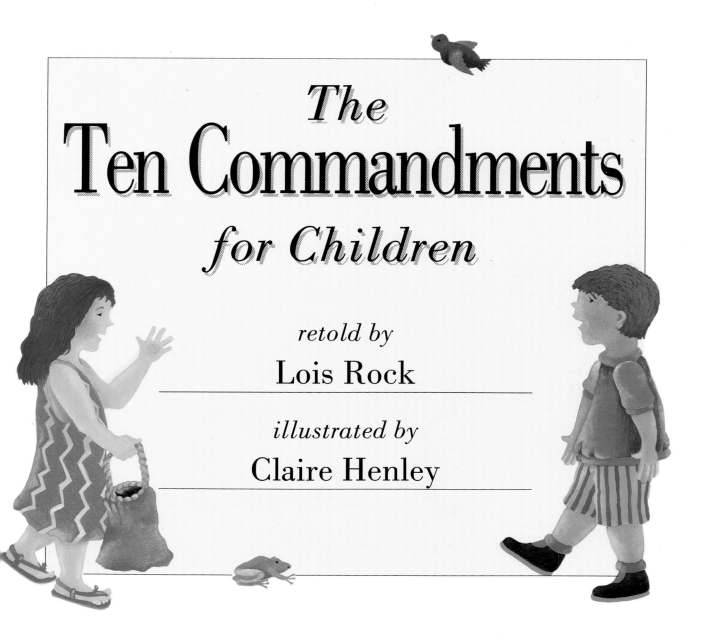

The
Ten Commandments
for Children

retold by

Lois Rock

illustrated by

Claire Henley

Text by Lois Rock
Copyright © 1995 Lion Publishing
Illustrations copyright © 1995 Claire Henley

The author asserts the moral right
to be identified as the author of this work

Published by
Lion Publishing
850 North Grove Avenue, Elgin, Illinois 60120, USA
ISBN 0 7459 3055 7

First edition 1995

Acknowledgments
The wording of the Ten Commandments at the end of this
book has been adapted from the version printed in
The Alternative Service Book 1980, which is adapted
from the version prepared by the International
Consultation on English Texts (ICET), and is reproduced
by permission of The Central Board of Finance of the
 Church of England.

Library of Congress CIP Data applied for

Printed and bound in Singapore

The Ten Commandments

From the beginning, the Bible says, the good and right way for people to live is to love the God who made them and to love one another.

This good and right way to live is set out in the Ten Commandments. These were laws that God gave a group of people called the Israelites thousands of years ago as they traveled from Egypt, where they had been slaves, to a land where they could be free: free to live as God wants.

You can find the story of the Israelites' escape from Egypt in the second book of the Bible—the book of Exodus. The Ten Commandments are in chapter 20, verses 1 to 17.

The God who gave these commandments is loving and kind. Today, as then, the people who respond to that love by obeying them will find joy and happiness.

I am God. I have always taken care of my people. You must love and obey me and no other gods.

Long ago, people called the Israelites were slaves in Egypt. The cruel king made them work and work building him new cities. They were very unhappy. But God loved those people and had a plan for them. So nothing went right for the king till he let the Israelites go.

Then they were free to find a new home, free to serve the God who had rescued them.

Dear God
You are loving and kind.
You help those who
are hurting. So I want to
follow your plans,
to live as you want.

Don't let anything be more important than me.

The Israelites knew that God could be trusted— because God had rescued them. Other nations made models of their gods from wood and stone and prayed to them. They made them more important than the living God who made the whole world and takes care of it.

Dear God
You are the maker
of all things.
I put my trust in you.

You must respect me, and take care how you speak about me.

We must always remember that God is in charge of us and of the whole world.

Dear God
You are greater and wiser than I am.
I want to treat you with respect.

Keep my day of rest, one special day each week.

From the beginning
God made people
to enjoy six busy days
and then a day of rest.

Dear God
You want people
to enjoy your world.
Thank you
for your day of rest.

Show respect to your mother and father.

There are good times with your mother and father when loving them is easy.
And there are other times when you feel cross.
But families are meant to love and help each other at all times.

Dear God
You are kind and loving whatever we have done.
I want to find good ways to show that kind of love to my parents.

Do not murder.

It's good to be alive:
to work and play,
to eat and sleep,
to laugh and cry,
to love and be loved.

Dear God
You give us life and you
take care of us.
I want to take care of
people too, and
never, never
harm or hurt them.

Husbands and wives: keep your special love just for each other.

Friends love and trust one another.
Husbands and wives promise to be special friends for ever.
When a friend is loyal and kind, love and happiness grow.

Dear God
I want to learn now to be loyal and kind and stay that way when I grow up.

Do not steal.

We may like
something
that belongs to
someone else
but we know
it's not fair
just to take it.

Dear God
I want to trust you
for the things I need.

Do not tell lies.

How sad it is when someone tells lies about you.
People who tell lies cannot trust each other.
Then they can't be good friends and it's hard to put right whatever has gone wrong.

Dear God
I want to tell the truth,
so my friends can trust me,
and together we can work
to help put things right.

Do not be greedy for the things other people have.

Some people
have so much more
than we do.
We want
good things too!

Dear God
You are generous
and kind.
Help me to have fun
and be happy
with what you have
given me.

1. I am God. I have always taken care of my people. You must love and obey me and no other gods.
2. Don't let anything be more important than me.
3. You must respect me, and take care how you speak about me.
4. Keep my day of rest, one special day each week.
5. Show respect to your mother and father.
6. Do not murder.
7. Husbands and wives: keep your special love just for each other.
8. Do not steal.
9. Do not tell lies.
10. Do not be greedy for the things other people have.

1. God spoke all these words, saying, I am the Lord your God, who brought you out of the land of Egypt... You shall have no other gods before me.

2. You shall not make for yourself graven images... you shall not bow down to them or serve them...

3. You shall not take the name of the Lord your God in vain.

4. Remember the sabbath day, to keep it holy.

5. Honor your father and your mother.

6. You shall not kill.

7. You shall not commit adultery.

8. You shall not steal.

9. You shall not bear false witness against your neighbor.

10. You shall not covet anything that is your neighbor's.